D1094931

CHERUBINI

Oxford Studies of Composers

General Editor : Colin Mason

Egon Wellesz: FUX

Denis Arnold: MARENZIO

Basil Deane: CHERUBINI

Oxford Studies of Composers (*3*)

CHERUBINI

BASIL DEANE

London
OXFORD UNIVERSITY PRESS
NEW YORK   TORONTO
1965

Oxford University Press, Amen House, London E.C.4

GLASGOW NEW YORK TORONTO MELBOURNE WELLINGTON
BOMBAY CALCUTTA MADRAS KARACHI LAHORE DACCA
CAPE TOWN SALISBURY NAIROBI IBADAN
KUALA LUMPUR HONG KONG

ACKNOWLEDGEMENTS

I should like to express my appreciation to Dr. V. Politi, Director of the Italian Cultural Institute in Melbourne, for his interest in this book, and to thank the Italian Government for their generous travel award. I owe a debt of gratitude to the staff at the library of the Conservatorio Luigi Cherubini in Florence for their kindly assistance to a new-comer, and to the officials of the music department of the BibliothèqueNationale in Paris, who offered me their customary courteous and efficient co-operation.

*Printed in Great Britain
by W. & J. Mackay & Co. Ltd.
Chatham, Kent*

INTRODUCTION

BIOGRAPHICAL and critical attention to Cherubini has reflected the varying fortunes of his music over more than a century. The primary source of information about the oeuvre is the composer's own *Catalogue général par ordre chronologique*. This record was kept meticulously by Cherubini until 1839, three years before his death. It was first published, with the last works included in a supplement, in 1843. Reproduced in several nineteenth-century biographies, it also forms the basis of the valuable *Chronologisches Verzeichnis der Werke Luigi Cherubinis unter Kennzeichnung der in der Musikabteilung der Berliner Staatsbibliothek erhaltenen Handschriften*, by C. Schröder, published in the *Beiträge zur Musikwissenschaft* (Berlin, 1962). The decades following the composer's death saw the publication of several important biographies: in Italy, the *Notizie* of Picchianti, 1843; in France, *Cherubini, sa vie, ses oeuvres, son rôle artistique*, by A. Pougin, serialized in *Le Ménestrel* from 1881 to 1882; in England, *Cherubini, Memorials illustrative of his life*, by E. Bellasis (1874), useful mainly for biographical and bibliographical detail, and for its inclusion of Cherubini's *Catalogue*.

After 1882 interest steadily declined in most countries. The brief studies by Bennet (1883) and Crowest (1890) are of slight importance, and there has been nothing of note in English since. (The Cherubini Society, however, has done fine work in making recordings of the music available.) France has produced nothing further since Pougin. Germany, whose record of Cherubini performance surpasses that of her neighbours, entered the field late, but made up for the delay by the quality of her contribution. *Luigi Cherubini, Sein Leben und seine Werke*, by R. H. Hohenemser (Leipzig, 1913), is the first critical and aesthetic assessment of the music, based on a close analysis of the scores. Excellent in its detail, its main weakness is a doubtless unconscious desire on the part of its author to assimilate the composer into a specifically German tradition. Hohenemser's work was extended by L. Schemann in his *Cherubini* (Stuttgart, 1925). Schemann's enthusiasm for his subject is epitomized by his comparison of Cherubini's achievement with those of his fellow Florentines Dante and Michelangelo. Nevertheless, his book, excellently documented, is penetrating in its relation of the composer's music to his personality and historical background.

For years his native country neglected Cherubini. Guido Confalonieri's two-volume work, *Prigionia di un artista. Il romanzo di Luigi Cherubini*, published in Milan in 1948, was a magnificent rectification, contributing much to the awakening of interest in the composer in Italy. Imaginative scholarship and critical acumen are blended in an outstanding study of the composer, an indispensable source of information and ideas for any serious student of Cherubini. Finally, the symposium *Luigi Cherubini nel il centenario della nascita*, edited by Alberto Damerini (Florence, 1962), deals with various aspects of the composer's career. It is especially valuable for three contributions: a detailed investigation of the early Florentine period by Mario Fabbri; the modestly entitled 'Tentativo di un Catalogo della produzione di Luigi Cherubini' by François Lesure and Claudio Sartori, which, despite some minor errors, is the most complete and accurate catalogue so far prepared, including as it does the dates of composition and first performance, whereabouts of extant manuscripts, and principal editions; and a useful critical biography by Mariangela Donà.

A full-length study in English is now overdue. Meanwhile, this book is intended as a general introduction to the composer's music. Since Cherubini wrote more than 430 compositions in the course of a long life, some selection is inevitable. I have been guided in my choice by two sometimes conflicting considerations: the desirability of offering an overall view of Cherubini's musical personality in an historical perspective and the intrinsic importance of individual compositions. Where scores are readily available, as, for instance, in the case of the major church works and the overtures, I have allowed myself some more detailed analysis. I have included the overtures in the chapter on orchestral music because they are independent compositions in their own right, and are, in fact, most often heard in concert performance.

CHAPTER ONE

THEATRE MUSIC

I T was understandable that Cherubini, whose father was harpsichordist at the Teatro alla Pergola in Florence, should be directed towards opera composition, the surest path to fame and fortune in eighteenth-century Italy. That he should be accepted as a pupil and assistant by Giuseppe Sarti in 1778, before he was 18, was a promising start to his career. Sarti was regarded as one of the leading representatives of the second Neapolitan school, and during Cherubini's youth his opere serie were in great demand, both in Italy and abroad. His work was typical of the school, in its qualities and limitations. The three acts of the Metastasian texts were set to music whose overriding characteristic was its melodic grace and whose prime function was to provide a vehicle of display for virtuoso singers. The aria dominated the structure; the older 'da capo' form had given place to the two-section aria, which at least allowed a modicum of psychological evolution. Ensembles were restricted to the duet at the end of the first act, the trio that terminated the second act, and a larger ensemble or chorus to conclude the work. The harmonic vocabulary and the orchestration were rudimentary. The limited range of the formal, melodic, and harmonic clichés which made up the idiom virtually eliminated even involuntary originality, and stifled any genuine response to the dramatic content of the stereotyped libretti.

In his first ten operas Cherubini showed himself an apt pupil. His settings of such currently familiar texts as *Il Quinto Fabio*, *Armida abbandonata*, *Mesenzio re d'Etruria*, *Il Giulio Sabino*, *Ifigenia in Aulide*, are at first sight indistinguishable from those of his contemporaries. He accepted the idiom without question and quickly mastered its techniques. But a closer examination of these unpublished manuscripts reveals some personal preferences within the conventions. His contemporaries lavished their greatest care on the arias, treating the rest of the opera in a more or less perfunctory manner. Cherubini appears to be more interested in the ensembles, which he expands by changes of tempo and time signature; and he handles the recitative with a genuine regard for its expressive possibilities. It is perhaps in his use of the orchestra that his personality begins to emerge most clearly. Whenever the text permits a dramatic treatment Cherubini relies on his orchestra to intensify the effect, and the orchestration of the last two opere serie, *Il Giulio Sabino* and *Ifigenia in Aulide*, is much richer than was customary at the time.

But opera seria, frozen in its own absurdities, was doomed, and not even Mozart could save it. So it was a happy chance that led Cherubini to seek his fortune in Paris, where he took up residence with the violinist Viotti in 1788, after a brief visit to London. For an opera composer Paris was at that time the most exciting city in the world. The reverberations of the Gluck-Piccinni dispute were still echoing in literary and musical circles. Several composers had been asserting their claim to the master's vacant title: Piccinni himself, Gluck's pupil Salieri, and Sacchini. None had secured his position, and the arrival of a young Italian composer who had won a reputation for himself in his own country was therefore an event of importance. During his stay in London Cherubini had already begun work on a libretto by Marmontel, Piccinni's sometime collaborator and a leader of the anti-Gluck faction. This opera, *Démophon*, was performed at the end of 1788. It was, by general agreement, a failure. 'If words make an opera, *Démophon* is an opera,' said one wit, with more conciseness than clarity. And its fate was sealed when a rival version by Vogel was acclaimed in the following year.

In retrospect it is easy to see that failure was inevitable. Marmontel based his French libretto on Metastasio, but sacrificed his predecessor's directness by introducing a superfluous sub-plot. Diffuse in structure, his text is pompously banal in language. Cherubini had the task of adapting his native style to a language which he barely knew, one whose sounds and intellectual content are inseparable. Moreover, he had seen and appreciated Gluck's work, and was endeavouring to reconcile his idiom with the principles of reform opera as far as possible. The results are at times ludicrous. For the sake of melodic continuity and motivic development in the accompaniment Cherubini commits verbal repetitions barely conceivable in Italian, intolerable in French. In the duet between Osmide and Dircé in the second act the text runs thus:

Oui pour jamais oui pour jamais il est à toi ce coeur malheureux qu'on déchire ce coeur malheureux ce coeur malheureux qu'on déchire soit que je vive ou que j'expire soit que je vive ou que j'expire oui pour jamais il est à toi il est à toi etc.

Such treatment, and the frequent false accentuations, would hardly be acceptable to a public who judged an opera first of all as a setting of a libretto.

With all its weaknesses, however, *Démophon* has real qualities, even if they do not justify Schemann's claim that this is the first French music-drama. The very obstacles confronting Cherubini, the necessity to learn new techniques, acted as a liberating force for his dramatic instincts. His melodic line is no longer governed by the suave regularity of the Italian school. At its best it springs from the psychological situation and the textual rhythm, and acquires a new amplitude, as in the expression of the rage of King Astor (Ex. 1). The rigid distinction

Ex.1

between recitative and aria is broken down by accompanied recitative and arioso. The chorus plays a major part in the opera, from the opening scene of the work onwards (Ex. 2).

Ex.2

3

If Cherubini is indebted to Gluck for his example here, it is rather to Haydn that he owes his orchestral inspiration. His acquaintance with the Haydn symphonies in the mid-1780s was a revelation, and laid the foundation of his lifelong reverence for the Austrian composer. The purely instrumental movements in *Démophon*—the overture, the introduction to the second act, the marches and the ballets—show for the first time his gifts as an orchestral writer.

In 1789 Viotti and the influential Léonard, perfumer to the Queen, obtained a licence to open a theatre for Italian opera. The company assembled by Viotti was placed under the patronage of the Comte de Provence, and became known as the 'Troupe de Monsieur'. Cherubini was appointed musical director, and the additional numbers which he wrote for insertion into the comedies of Paisiello, Cimarosa, and others contributed to the very great success of the company. But the turn of political events, and the consequent departure of most of the Italian artists, wrought a change. The 'Troupe de Monsieur' moved to the Théâtre Feydeau, engaged French performers, and included in its repertoire some French opéras comiques, thus entering into direct competition with the official Opéra comique in the Rue Favart.

From its beginnings in the mid-eighteenth century opéra comique had marked itself off from opera buffa by its spoken dialogue, strophic songs, concluding vaudevilles, and by a much stronger emphasis on the pastoral and sentimental than on the purely comic elements. Grétry's popular *Richard Coeur de Lion* (1784) introduced the themes of rescue and heroism, and the difference between opéra comique and the productions of the Opéra national became increasingly one of form and setting rather than spirit, the term opéra comique being applied to any composition with spoken dialogue instead of recitative, regardless of subject-matter. It was against this background that Cherubini composed his next opera *Lodoiska*, a 'comédie héroique en trois actes'. The action, set in Poland, is typical of the 'rescue opera' type. The hero, Florensky, and his servant Varbel, aided by Titzikan and his band of savage but noble Tartars, finally succeed in rescuing the heroine, Lodoiska, from the clutches of the treacherous Durlinsky.

Lodoiska was performed at the Feydeau in 1791, and scored an immediate success. At the final curtain the ageing Grétry himself joined with those who bore the composer from the orchestral pit on to the stage, and thanked him publicly 'in the name of art'. His judgement was confirmed by the audiences, who applauded two hundred successive performances, and by the critics. The *Almanach général des spectacles* for 1792 declared, 'Never have French ears heard music that is more

4

characteristic and expressive.' And indeed *Lodoiska* represented an entirely new departure in opera. Despite its external similarities to some of its predecessors, notably *Richard Coeur de Lion*, it is entirely original in its depth of psychological insight, dramatic tension, and musical technique. In place of Grétry's arias and simple duets Cherubini employs a rich variety of formal structures. His numerous ensembles are used to carry forward the dramatic action, and his finales are similar in scope to those of Mozart (whose operas were unknown in France at that date). Grétry's harmony and texture are elementary. Cherubini uses his harmonic resources dramatically, and gives the orchestra an important role. Grétry's easy-going approach precludes penetration of character. Cherubini presents his characters with realism: the distinctions between the rough bravery of Titzikan, the persistence and fortitude of Florensky, and the more earthy preoccupations of Varbel are clearly established, and in her defiance of the tyrant and anxiety for her lover's safety Lodoiska is a tragic heroine.

Lodoiska opened a new path for opera composers, by demonstrating that areas of human experience outside the restricted fields of historical or mythological grand opera and comic opera could be treated seriously. In it Cherubini moves as far from the classical legends of Gluck as he does from the world of eighteenth-century comedy. Despite its geographically remote setting, the work was relevant to the turbulent world of the Revolution, and it set an example eagerly followed by such French composers as Méhul and Lesueur.

After Poland, Switzerland. In 1794 *Eliza ou le Mont Saint-Bernard*, a two-act opera with libretto by Saint-Cyr, was performed at the Feydeau. The action is simple, almost threadbare. Florindo, the hero, mistakenly believes that his Eliza has become betrothed to another. Accompanied by his servant Germain, he flees to the solitude of the Alps. There he is discovered by a prior and his monks, whose mission it is to succour lost travellers, and he is persuaded to rest in their hospice. Eliza and her companion Laura then arrive in the mountains, faint with fatigue, and they, too, are tended by the monks. Meanwhile, further false news has driven Florinda to despair, and he has disappeared into a raging blizzard, intending to end his life. Finally, and dramatically, he is rescued from an avalanche by the monks; the lovers are reunited, and all is explained. Although hampered by an indifferent libretto, Cherubini wrote some of his finest stage music on this occasion. A child of his time in this, as in other ways, he had a deep love of the beauty and isolation of nature, and he responded fully to the atmosphere of the setting. The outward calm of the mountain and its underlying menace are both conveyed in the opening scene (Exx. 3 and 4). The evocation of the onset of night, with the monastery bell tolling in the distance, at the end of the first act, is one of the first and most beautiful instances of that 'musique d'effet' so much abused by some of Cheru-

Ex.3

Ex.4

bini's successors. In contrast, the horror of the tempest in the second act is vividly depicted in the orchestra (Ex. 5).

Because of his renunciation of the Italian melodic style in *Démophon* and *Lodoïska* Cherubini was accused of lacking any gift for melody, and this charge has been repeated often enough since then. He did, in fact, have melodic ability, and when melody could serve a dramatic function he used it fully, as in the introduction to Scene 6 of Act I, in which the heroine is first presented. An expressive horn solo (Ex. 6) is accompanied lightly by strings. It would take us beyond the scope of this study to discuss in detail Cherubini's melodic idiom and its relation to the non-Italianate styles of Berlioz and Wagner respectively. But his strong preference for unequal phrase lengths, exemplified here, is a most important ingredient.

Weber, a fervent admirer and practical supporter of Cherubini, had a special (and understandable) affection for *Eliza*. Germain's air in

Ex. 5

Ex. 6

Act I, Scene 2 (Ex. 7), appears to be the direct inspiration for Aenn-chen's arietta in *Der Freischütz*. Its intimacy of feeling, its sensitive presentation of simple people face to face with the beauty, mystery, and terror of nature, support Confalonieri's claim that *Eliza*, written seven years before Chateaubriand's *Atala*, is the first manifesto of French romanticism.

7

Mais à sa bel - le__ on est fi - dè - le__ mais à__ sa belle on est fi - dè - le Vé-nus mê - me Vé-nus mê - me Vé-nus mê-me n'y pour-rait rien

Cherubini's next opera, *Médée*, had its première in March 1797, again at the Théâtre Feydeau. For his source, the librettist Hoffmann went to the drama of Pierre Corneille, who had himself been influenced by Seneca's treatment of the myth. Corneille had already dealt with the early stages of the story in his *Toison d'Or*, so that he was able in *Médée* to concentrate on the culmination of the tragedy, Medea's arrival in Corinth at the moment of Jason's intended marriage to the daughter of King Creon. Hoffmann, covering the same ground, was obliged to refer to preceding events in the course of the text, thus holding up the action. A further handicap to the composer was the opéra comique tradition of spoken dialogue. In the two earlier operas this restriction was merely unfortunate. In *Médée* it may be called tragic. At some of the most dramatic moments of the work, such as the first encounter between Medea and Jason, points where his skill in accompanied recitative would have enabled him to intensify the expression and give musical unity to the action, Cherubini had to stand aside and let the stilted lines of Hoffmann speak for themselves. This discontinuity has contributed to the neglect of the work. Yet the alternative was perhaps even worse. If the composition had been destined for the Opéra national, Cherubini would have been compelled to resolve the action in a concluding ballet and a happy ending, an unthinkable contradiction of his whole conception. Nowhere more than here was Cherubini the victim of the limiting theatrical conventions of his day.

The outstanding characteristic of *Médée* is its Racinian intensity, unprecedented and almost unparalleled in later operatic history. Nothing is allowed to distract attention from the tortured Medea, wife of Jason and descendant of Hecate, betrayed woman and avenging goddess, a mother driven by her husband's treachery to slay her own children. Cherubini's Medea is not that of Corneille, Seneca or even Euripides. No ratiocination, no psychological explanations veil the horror of the primitive myth. In order to realize his conception, the composer strips his vocabulary of everything that is merely decorative, or purely musical in effect. On the foundation of his earlier experiments he develops a dramatic melodic idiom of great expressive potential, and fraught with implications for the future, projecting the mental torment of Medea into the physical strain imposed on the singer by the tessitura, intervallic shape and dynamic range of the vocal line. He employs a whole gamut of devices to prevent the music from detaching itself from the dramatic situation: sudden interruptions of phrases, unexpected pauses, ostinato chord repetitions, extreme dynamic contrasts, fluctuations of tempo, new orchestral sounds and colours. It is not surprising that he is not always successful, and that some of his effects startle rather than convince. In view of the originality of his conception, it is indeed remarkable that the score achieves such a high degree of coherence and sureness.

After the powerful overture, Act I opens with the preparations for the wedding of Dircé, Creon's daughter, with Jason. The march accompanying the entry of the Argonauts surpasses, in its stately ceremonial, some better-known later examples. Jason attempts to dissipate Dircé's forebodings, and principals and chorus join in a prayer to the gods for their blessing on the forthcoming nuptials. At this point Medea enters. She curses Jason, and Creon in his wrath pronounces sentence of banishment on her in an aria which is a magnificent expression of explosive rage. Medea, left alone with Jason, controls herself, and makes a final plea as mother of his children to the indifferent Argonaut, in music of dignity and pathos (Ex. 8).

Ex.8

The course of the melody is several times interrupted by the exclamation 'ingrat!'. The Victorian critic Chorley's comment, quoted by Bellasis, is, though unimportant in itself, indicative of the gulf separating Cherubini from his public, both contemporary and posthumous. 'The abrupt cry, not to call it jerk, on the word "ingrat!" which finishes many of the phrases, and which unexpectedly starts out simultaneously with the last notes of the closing symphony, falls on English ears as one of those bit-by-bit settings of single words, which, however specious, are so false in point of art, whenever, as here, they interfere with the general spirit of the composition.' It is, of course, precisely because these exclamations 'interfere with the general spirit of the composition', revealing Medea's barely controlled anger, that Cherubini includes them. Jason's rejection of Medea's attempt at reconciliation leads to the concluding duet of the act containing the 'curse' motif (Ex. 9).

Ex.9

The introduction to the second act is a fine instance of Cherubini's dramatic treatment of the orchestra, and it prepares for Medea's hardening determination to wreak vengeance on Jason and his bride. Its similarity to the later *Egmont* overture is noteworthy (Ex. 10). In the

Ex.10

first scene Creon's refusal to allow Medea a postponement of the banishment decree provokes an outburst of concentrated fury (Ex. 11). Her maternal tenderness, which she has to conquer to complete her revenge, is poignantly betrayed in her farewell to her children in

Ex.11

Scene 5, not only by the vocal line, but also by the complementary motifs of the cellos and violins (Ex. 12). The closing scene of the second act is a superb example of the simultaneous presentation of event and commentary. Priests, warriors, people, led by Creon, Jason, and Dircé, enter the temple to invoke Hymen's blessing. Their prayers and hymns mingle with the wild imprecations of the listening Medea.

Ex.12

In its continuity and dramatic concentration, as well as its sense of inexorable doom, the third act matches the last act of *Otello*. The introduction, a 'temporale', is followed by a scena for Medea, still torn between love of her children and desire for revenge. The aria 'Du trouble affreux qui me dévore' is one of the most taxing in the repertoire. In the final scene Cherubini is driven to break the rule of spoken dialogue, and opens with a powerful recitative. Her last scruples overcome, Medea gloats over the course of destruction. During the offstage discovery of Dircé's death, contrived by the sorceress, her voice, ferociously exultant, obliterates the cry of the chorus (Ex. 13). The expression of

Ex.13

Jason's dismay appears as a variant of the 'curse' motif. The semitonal motif in the accompaniment plays an important part throughout the scene (Ex. 14). Her children dead, Medea destroys the temple by fire, and disappears, surrounded by three Eumenides, before the eyes of the terrified crowd.

Ex.14

This necessarily brief account can do no more than hint at the originality and grandeur of a work 'which we musicians', remarked Brahms nearly a century later, 'regard among ourselves as the summit of dramatic music'.

After the high tragedy of *Médée* came three one-act comedies, *L'Hôtellerie portugaise* of 1798, and, in the following year, *La Punition* and *La Prisonnière*, this last in collaboration with Cherubini's young friend and disciple, Boieldieu. Of the three the first is outstanding, and it is undoubtedly the composer's best production in the comic genre. The action takes place in an inn near the frontier of Spain and Portugal, and the plot concerns the obstacles to the union of a young couple, set up deliberately by the girl's elderly guardian—who naturally wants to marry his ward himself—and inadvertently by the well-intentioned but misguided innkeeper. Although the libretto was criticized freely, it is no worse than many others of its kind, and, granted the improbable premises, carries the action forward smoothly, allowing ample scope for the composer.

The slightly exotic setting is vaguely alluded to by the introduction of the 'La Folia' theme in the overture, and the sparkling 'alla polacca' in the vaudeville finale. The other numbers include several romances and simple arias, a trio and a quartet, and show that Cherubini could rival his contemporaries when he wished in the field of comedy. The trio, like some of Mozart's ensembles, is a fully worked-out sonata form movement, and the solo numbers have a graceful melodic flow. Although the opera was never published, its musical qualities would certainly justify an occasional revival.

Cherubini began the new century auspiciously, with the greatest popular success of his career. His opera *Les deux Journées*, known in Germany as *Der Wasserträger* and in England as *The Watercarrier*, opened at the Feydeau in January 1800, and was accorded a tumultuous reception. Its fame and influence spread quickly throughout Europe, especially the German-speaking countries. Bellasis refers to a mangled English version entitled *The Escapes*, performed in 1801. Like so many of Cherubini's works it was ignored by his own countrymen. It did not reach Italy until 1942, although an Italian version was presented in London in 1872.

The scene is set in the France of Cardinal Mazarin, and concerns the rescue by a Savoyard watercarrier, Mikeli, aided by his children, of an aristocrat, Count Armand, who is being pursued by the agents of Mazarin for his part in the Fronde uprising. In the course of the rescue the Count is recognized as the man who once rendered a great service to Antonio, Mikeli's son. The text is by Bouilly, who was also responsible for the original *Léonore* on which *Fidelio* is based, and for the first and last time a libretto set by Cherubini won universal praise. Beethoven, asked to name the best libretti known to him, cited *La Vestale* and *Les deux Journées*. Mendelssohn proposed it, together with *Fidelio*, as a suitable model to the librettist Planché. Goethe who should have known better, considered it so perfect that it would be a success even if performed as a spoken play. In fact, Bouilly's text, like that of almost every other opera, could not possibly be staged without a musical setting.

Goethe and other contemporaries probably allowed their artistic judgement to be influenced by factors that were neither strictly musical nor dramatic. *Les deux Journées* is, as Schemann observed, a Volksoper. Through the motives and actions of its protagonists it offers an idealization of life, corresponding to the innermost desires of its audience, who can identify themselves easily with the characters and situations. The seventeenth-century background misled nobody. Whether or not there were Savoyard watercarriers in Mazarin's time was a matter which the audiences were content to leave to social historians. But these peasants who came from their mountains to ply their humble yet essential trade were familiar figures in late eighteenth-century Paris. (Savoyards in general were invested with a Rousseauesque romance, and appeared frequently—sometimes, as in *Eliza*, superfluously—on the stage.) And, in fact, the story was suggested to Bouilly by an incident which occurred during the Revolution.

In 1800 the events of the Reign of Terror were still vivid in the memories of the audience, but they were beginning to recede into perspective. The idealism which, however perverted, was one of the prime causes of the Revolution now took on a less militant aspect. Disinterested idealism is the mainspring of the action in *Les deux Journées*. The philosophy that moves Mikeli to risk his life in the rescue attempt is a simple humanitarian one:

> Non, il n'est point dans la nature
> De souvenir plus caressant
> Que celui qui tout bas murmure
> J'ai secouru, j'ai sauvé l'innocent.

The moral of the drama is expounded in the closing chorus:

> Et qu'aucun d'nous jamais n'oublie
> Que le premier charme de la vie
> Est de servir l'humanité.

At the same time a mood of social reconciliation pervaded the people, weary of internal bloodshed and attacked by enemies from without—a mood reflected in Napoleon's Constitution of 1799. And reconciliation between the classes is depicted in the opera by the juxtaposition of a count and a watercarrier, sharing a common danger, displaying the same qualities of courage, steadfastness, and fidelity.

14

Despite its topicality, the opera would not have achieved its success without a score of immediate popular appeal. The democratic nature of the plot is reflected in the musical structure. There is a predominance of ensembles. The only two solo numbers, Antonio's romance and Mikeli's aria, occur at the beginning of the opera, and both are directly tuneful in the opéra comique tradition (Exx. 15 and 16). These solos have, more-

Ex.15

over, a specific dramatic function as recurrent motifs. So, for instance, in the finale of Act I, Mikeli asks his daughter to remain in Paris in order to aid his plans: she demurs, and bursts into tears. The orchestra, playing *ff*, breaks off abruptly, and a solo clarinet plays the theme of Antonio's romance—what would later have been called the motif of gratitude. Marcellina, contrite, agrees to her father's scheme. 'This invariably produces a very great effect,' observed Weber, who was enraged by a performance at Monte Carlo in 1811 in which this motif was doubled by the oboe and accompanied.

The same fluent melodiousness characterizes some of the ensembles, as, for example, the 'choeur champêtre' of the third act (Ex. 17). The

Ex.17

scale and importance of the ensembles, particularly of the three finales, distinguish the musical style from that of earlier opéras comiques. So, too, does the well-conceived melodrama—instrumental background to spoken dialogue—used in the last two acts. Even if its significance has been exalted at the expense of his other compositions, *Les deux Journées* remains one of Cherubini's most attractive works, for its directness and sincerity.

The year of *Les deux Journées* was the high-water mark of Cherubini's career as an opera composer. The tide turned swiftly. *Anacréon ou l'amour fugitif*, staged at the Opéra in 1803, was a disaster, and closed after seven performances. Anacreon was a popular subject at the time. Grétry's *Anacréon chez Polycrate* had been successful a few years earlier, and Méhul had also worked on a version of the theme. But on this occasion Cherubini accepted a miserably inept libretto, which no musical excellence could salvage. This is particularly unfortunate, since the requirement of the theatre called for the inclusion of ballet music, and in the purely instrumental sections—the overture, the storm scene at the end of the first act, and the dance movements—Cherubini's inspiration is at its peak.

This failure contributed to the composer's increasing alienation from the stage. He was aware that the public, despite its acclaim for *Les deux Journées*, preferred the work of other musicians such as Boieldieu and Isouard. There were other grounds for concern. His beloved Théâtre Feydeau, to whose achievement he had given so much, was forced to close down. The mutual antipathy existing between Napoleon and himself excluded his work from official support or recognition. These factors, and the responsibility of maintaining his growing family, brought on attacks of nervous depression, and he withdrew as much as possible from the public eye. In 1805 a visit to Vienna, where he had many admirers, was a welcome interlude. He was well received in Viennese musical circles, and had the pleasure of paying homage in person to Haydn, who presented him with the manuscript of his 'Drum-roll' Symphony. During his stay he composed and supervised the production of *Faniska*, a rescue opera similar in theme to *Lodoïska*. Although the work was applauded at its first performance, and praised by Haydn and Beethoven, it was a succès d'estime. Yet again, Cherubini had set to music an impossible hotch-potch, with all the faults and none of the merits of *Lodoïska*.

The overwhelming reception accorded to Spontini's *La Vestale* in 1807 revealed to Cherubini the extent of the rift between himself and the French public. He was later to write other works for the stage, including two one-act operas: *Pimmalione* (1809, composed as a vehicle for Napoleon's favourite singer, the castrato Crescentini) and *Crescendo* (1810); *Les Abencérages* (1813), an attempt to compete with Spontini on his own ground of heroic grand opera; and *Ali Baba* (1833), a re-working of an early unperformed comedy, *Koukourgi*. But regardless of their diverse merits (and those of *Les Abencérages* are considerable), none of these works was destined to succeed. Meanwhile it seemed as if

Cherubini's career was finished. Morose and withdrawn, he virtually abandoned composition, and devoted himself to his serious recreations of painting and botany. It was with these studies in mind that he accepted an invitation in the spring of 1808 to visit an old acquaintance, the Princess of Chimay, at her estate near the Franco-Belgian border.

CHAPTER TWO

CHURCH MUSIC

THE facts about what took place at Chimay have often been told. The villagers, perhaps at the instigation of Cherubini's hostess, sent a deputation to ask him for a composition to perform in church on St. Cecilia's day. Cherubini abruptly declined, then changed his mind and wrote a Kyrie and part of a Gloria for the service. These events, however, do not in themselves explain his subsequent dedication to liturgical music, a dedication amounting to his virtual rebirth as a composer. He was already familiar with church music, having written a considerable quantity of it while under Sarti's guidance, and he had recently completed and published an eight-voice a cappella Credo, begun nearly thirty years earlier in emulation of his master, then put aside. But the early works are unremarkable, and the Credo is primarily an exercise in technique, while into the later compositions Cherubini put all the energy and emotion he had previously devoted to stage composition. He was certainly not seeking fortune or popularity; church music was scarcely a path to advancement in Imperial France. Nor does it appear likely that he had any new spiritual revelation. His religious life, entirely orthodox, was governed by his love of order. 'He was no mystic in religion,' affirmed his daughter. If religion was not a passion for Cherubini, music was. And it was probably his unwavering devotion to his art that led him to the realization that here, in the service of the liturgy, he could employ all his professional skills: his command of polyphony, his control of the orchestra, his insight into the implications of a text. Moreover his personal response to his theme—one more sublime and possibly more dramatic than those of the theatre—would no longer be exposed to the fickle taste of the opera-going public. On his return to Paris Cherubini resumed the work begun at Chimay, and the Mass in F, for three voices and orchestra, was completed in 1809.

The absence of a living tradition of Latin church music in France, and Cherubini's admiration for Haydn, might suggest the Masses of the Austrian composer as a model for this new form of composition. Certainly the main outlines of the Mass in F correspond to those of Haydn's settings. Like him, Cherubini divides the Gloria and Credo into several sections, contrasted in key and tempo. The Gloria and the Credo begin, and the Agnus Dei ends, quickly; while the Qui tollis, Crucifixus and beginning of the Agnus Dei are slow. He sets 'in gloria Dei' and 'et vitam venturi' as fugues, and uses soloists in the Benedictus. But it is not necessary to postulate a direct imitation in order to explain these similarities. Such features were part of the common eighteenth-century heritage. Cherubini was brought up in a branch of the tradition different from that of the Austrians, who were influenced by the Neapolitan school in their borrowings from operatic techniques and by the Venetians in their orchestral colouring. Through Sarti he inherited the more austere outlook of Padre Martini and the Roman school, who condemned instrumental and vocal display in liturgical music. In the F major Mass, Cherubini's vocal style is less florid, his instrumental support less decorative than Haydn's. And, broadly speaking, his music reflects more closely the meaning of the liturgy.

The clearest influence of Sarti's instruction may be seen in the fugues. As well as the concluding sections of the Gloria and the Credo, traditionally fugal, Cherubini sets the 'Christe eleison' as a fugue. With one or two exceptions, his fugal movements are the least satisfactory part of his church music. The academic eighteenth-century fugue, valuable as it was for contrapuntal training, was a stereotyped composition. The form did not arise out of the material, as in Bach's work, but moulded it. So each of the fugues in this Mass is constructed to the same standard pattern, with exposition in double counterpoint, middle entries in progressively closer stretto, extended dominant pedal before the final entries. The subjects are drawn from the common eighteenth-century pool (Exx. 18, 19, and 20). The facile flow of Cherubini's technique causes him to forget the expressive aim of the music, and the

Ex.18

Allegretto

Chris - te   e - le - i - son   e - le - i - son

Ex.19

Allegro

In   glo - ri - a   De - i   Pat - ris

Ex.20

Presto

Et   vi - tam ven - tu - ri,   et   vi - tam

proportion of the fugues to the surrounding movements. Thus the 'Christe' section of the Kyrie is too prolonged, and breaks the unity of the whole.

The simple diatonic harmony of the fugues also forms the basis of the strong homophonic sections, such as the opening of the Gloria. At other times the desire to increase the expressive content of his music leads Cherubini to experiment with chromaticism. Sometimes these chromatic progressions are directly related to the text, as at the 'Crucifixus', where the hushed voices, accompanied by gently sustained harmony and pizzicato strings, convey the solemnity of the text (Ex. 21).

Ex.21

Elsewhere the textual justification for the chromaticisms is less obvious, as in this passage from the Gloria, 'Deus Pater' (Ex. 22). An effect of

Ex.22

purely musical contrast occurs in the 'Quoniam'. This section begins with a strong unison theme, supported by full orchestra (Ex. 23).

Ex.23

Abruptly the *ff* changes to *pp*, and on a repetition of the text 'Tu solus dominus' Ex. 24 ensues. Only the most sophisticated theological interpretation could justify this change of meaning. The two harmonic

Ex.24

poles of the work are posited in the introduction to the Kyrie, where the diatonic opening and closing bars frame a variety of chromatic progressions (Ex. 25).

Ex.25

If the artistic sins of the children are to be visited on the fathers, then the frequent juxtaposition in some of Cherubini's church music of unadorned rudimentary diatonic progressions and chromatic harmonies often based on the diminished seventh puts him in a particularly vulnerable position. Of the attendant dangers, dullness and sentimentality, Cherubini escapes the second, if not always the first. Certain of his Victorian successors were less fortunate. His superb sense of orchestral colour helped to strengthen and enliven his idiom. Thus, in the Credo, the *ff* unison of the trumpets and horns on a single note conjures up a vision of judgement before the 'judicare vivos', and the soft tone of the flute and clarinets enhance the gentle pleading of the first 'miserere nobis'. On occasion the orchestral accompaniment plays the leading role in the thematic development (and here, perhaps, Cherubini is indebted to his Austrian predecessors). The opening Allegro moderato of the Credo is of symphonic proportions, 138 bars long. The voices expound a cantus firmus, while the orchestra develops three complementary thematic fragments. The overall form is close to sonata form, with exposition, development, and varied recapitulation. A feature of the Credo is the frequent return of the word 'credo' itself, set to a descending fifth, in the course of the text, a procedure adopted by Mozart in K. 257 and by Beethoven in the Missa Solemnis.

Long as the Mass in F is, its proportions are exceeded by those of the Mass in D minor of 1811, whose total length is greater than that of Beethoven's masterpiece. This scale excludes it from any liturgical use, and militates against concert performance. It is, however, the most interesting of the ordinary Masses. In the Mass in F Cherubini was perhaps overconscious of the weight of tradition, and curbed his dramatic instinct. Here he works more boldly, on a larger canvas, making full use of dynamic and colour contrasts. His forces are enlarged; he writes for the normal four-part chorus, and his orchestra includes full double woodwind, horns, trumpets, trombones, timpani and strings. He divides the five sections of the Gloria and Credo respectively into separate movements, and adopts a slightly more florid style of vocal writing for the soloists, illustrated in an extract from 'Gratias agimus' (Ex. 26).

Ex.26

The application of traditional technique to expressive purpose on a broad scale is illustrated in the third petition of the Kyrie, set as a fugue. The subject, with its quiet undulation, its supple syncopation, is rich in potentiality (Ex. 27). Cherubini begins with an exposition whose tranquil vocal lines are lightly accompanied by the orchestra. A note of urgency is introduced by a stretto with chromatic movement; but the

Ex.27

22

dynamic level remains *pp* for the whole of this section of sixty-seven bars. The next section begins *f*, and expounds a shortened inversion of the subject, again in stretto. After a homophonic climax, a diminuendo leads to the final section. This begins softly with the abbreviated subject in the original position, developed in closer stretto (Ex. 28). The culmination of this section is a descending chromatic passage, with

Ex. 28

Ex. 29

syncopated dynamics (Ex. 29). Finally the fugue resolves into a brief reminiscence of the opening Kyrie, again *pp*. So the prayer develops from the quiet humility of the opening, through the stronger plea of the middle section and the anguished cry of the chromatic progression to the return of the opening mood in the final utterance.

The scale of the 'Crucifixus' is also increased, and with the same interpretative intention. For fifty bars the voices intone the text on a repeated E. In the orchestra the muted violins weave an arabesque, the bass strings, trombones, and timpani reiterate an ominous rhythmic figure, and the woodwind interject short melodic phrases (Ex. 30). Other movements deserving of attention are the dramatically conceived 'Qui tollis' and the Agnus Dei. The Sanctus and the Benedictus, as often with Cherubini, are less inspired.

The Mass in D minor was not composed with any performance, liturgical or otherwise, in view. The later Masses, including the Mass in C major (1816), and the two Coronation Masses, G major (1819) and A major (1825), date from Cherubini's years as Superintendent of the Chapel Royal, and were all intended for church use. They differ from the customary pattern by the substitution of an O salutaris for an independent Benedictus, and some include an offertory. They are shorter in length than the two earlier Masses, and as a result are musically less satisfying.

More interesting than these later Masses are the motets composed for the Chapel Royal. These range from large-scale works for chorus and orchestra in several sections to short solos with string accompaniment, and, as might be expected, they display much greater stylistic diversity than the Masses. A typical example of the more extended motet is the *Regina Coeli* of 1817. This is in three movements; the central minor Lento is framed by two major sections, containing powerful vocal writing and a brilliant use of the orchestra to communicate the jubilation of the hymn.

Equally fine are the *Inclina Domine*, in four movements, and the *Confirma hoc Deus*, for three voices and orchestra, composed for the coronation of Charles X in Rheims Cathedral. Settings for a trio of soloists include an *Adoremus* for three equal voices, in canon, and a graceful *Ave verum* for women's voices (Ex. 31). Among the solo

Ex.31

motets some, like the extensive *O fons amoris* for tenor with choral accompaniment, or the shorter *O salutaris* for solo alto with strings, are spoilt by excessive fioriture in the solo line. The *Venite* for bass, on the other hand, has a majestic dignity. The best known of these solos is the *Ave Maria* for soprano, cor anglais, and strings. The music conveys the tender pleading of the prayer. Modulation and chromaticism express an undercurrent of anxiety; but it is the serenity of the opening which finally prevails (Ex. 32). It is unfortunate that this should be the only

Ex. 32

example of Cherubini's church music to be generally known, especially since it is frequently performed with that excess of sentimentality which passes in many circles for religious conviction.

Excellent as many of the motets are, they are overshadowed by those twin peaks, the two Requiems. The Requiem in C minor was commissioned by the Government in 1815, for the anniversary commemoration in the following year of the execution of Louis XVI. At the time the composer's fortunes were at their zenith. The Restoration brought a political régime which was in accordance with his own ideas, and gave him the recognition he had long been denied. He was for the first time financially secure, and his domestic life, always happy, was enriched by the engagement of his eldest daughter to a young man who had won his warm approval. His own tranquillity, and the nature of the occasion —the commemoration not only of a dead monarch, but of the thousands whose deaths were symbolized by that of Louis—caused him to aim at a setting which would have a universal application. He had already had an opportunity to reflect upon the meaning of the Requiem Mass and the musician's approach to it, for it was he who first introduced Mozart's Requiem to France, in 1805. Though he revered Mozart, however, Cherubini was little influenced by him in the C minor Requiem.

It was essential to his conception that everything of an apparently restricting nature should be suppressed, and that no detail should distract from the overall unity. He therefore cut out soloists entirely. He strove for continuous, cohesive forms, and distilled his musical idiom, omitting any embellishment of the melodic lines and relating his chromaticism and modulation strictly to the textual meaning. In the vocal score his setting looks bare to the point of naïveté. In performance, when the orchestra colours the chords and lines, when the dynamic proportions and the formal structure are realized in sound, it comes alive, direct in its impact, utterly convincing in its interpretation of the liturgy.

The Introit establishes the authority of the entire work. A brief unison phrase in the lower strings and bassoons, repeated and expanded, leads into the first choral entry, *pp* (Ex. 33). At 'te decet

Ex.33

hymnus' a new motif, again of elemental simplicity, is taken up by the voices, still *pp* (Ex. 34). On the text 'exaudi orationem meam' a crescendo to a chord of A♭ minor expresses unease and suspense.

Ex.34

These are dissolved in the calm of the following A♭ major progression (Ex. 35). Once more only do the voices rise above *pp*, and the resolution of the opening phrase into a C major chord ends the movement.

Ex.35

The Graduale, in G minor, is a quiet movement, only twenty bars in length. It begins by developing an antiphonal dialogue between the voices grouped in pairs. At the end they unite in a cadence with another major resolution.

The Dies irae, with its vision of the Day of Judgement—the dead rising at the last trump, the judgement seat, the separation of righteous and unrighteous, the flames of hell, the fervently repeated pleas for mercy—has always been for composers the central text of the Requiem Mass. It lends itself to vivid musical imagery and the strongest contrasts. Fauré found it too dramatic, and reduced it to a minor episode. But other composers, notably Mozart, Berlioz and Verdi, have split it into independent movements, dwelling upon the pictorial opportunities of the Tuba mirum, the operatic scope of the Recordare. In each case the overall unity of the medieval hymn has been lost, its meaning obscured by its symbolism. Cherubini sets the Dies irae in one continuous movement, thus interweaving, as they are interwoven in the text, the two complementary themes of judgement and redemption.

A repeated G, *ff*, and a single stroke of the gong, are the prelude to the hymn. Against a background of scurrying violins the choir enunciate the text, quietly, men answering women (Ex. 36). The voices come

Ex.36

together in a crescendo which reaches a *f* chord of G major, and reiterated Gs in the brass resolve into the strong statement of 'Tuba mirum' (Ex. 37). A temporary change of expression occurs at 'Mors

Ex.37

stupebit,' the vocal parts becoming quiet and staccato. With 'Liber scriptus' Cherubini resumes his opening idea (Ex. 36), beginning now in E♭ major, and 'Rex tremendae' is set to the same music as 'Tuba

C.–C

mirum' (Ex. 37). A move to C major comes with the prayer 'Salva me' (Ex. 38). Out of this melodic descent Cherubini evolves an orchestral motif which forms the background to the next part of the text, 'Recordare'. 'Dolce assai', but without any sentimentality, the voices in turn make their plea. A crescendo leads to the excitement of 'Confutatis

Ex.38

maledictus' (Ex. 39). The music of 'Salva me' (Ex. 38) returns with the words 'voca me', and is followed by a subdued 'Oro supplex' with a notable use of a pedal C in the accompaniment. From 'Lacrimosa' the voices move together, in penitence, the anxiety of the text and of the *fp* chords resolving after the third 'Amen' into the serene assurance of C major.

Ex.39

The Offertorium is in E♭ major, with the predictable move to the minor for 'de poenis infernis.' The chromaticism of this first part is dispelled by the B♭ major of 'sed signifer sanctus Michael'. The three upper voices, accompanied by the higher instruments of the orchestra, create a sound of luminous beauty to match the text. With 'Quam olim Abrahae' Cherubini bows to tradition and writes a fugue. It is a finely executed example on a strong subject, but it is out of place in this work, where the music is otherwise so strictly a function of the text. The 'Hostias' is an offering of grace and delicate vocal and orchestral colour, beginning in C major and moving through a range of keys before coming to rest on the dominant chord of Eb major. A repetition of the fugue ends the movement.

The Sanctus (Ab major) is short, and is the most conventional and least distinguished part of the score. The Pie Jesu (F minor), on the other hand, has a strange originality and unusual harmonic flavour. The sopranos' opening phrase (Ex. 40), is followed by a variant for clarinets and bassoons (Ex. 41). Later the melody is restated by all the choir (Ex. 42) and the instrumental version concludes this quiet, impersonal movement.

The culmination of the setting is the final Agnus Dei. A short string phrase leads to the choral entry (Ex. 43). In each statement the invocation 'Agnus Dei' is made strongly, the prayer 'dona eis requiem' softly. A central climax is succeeded by a prolonged decrescendo of unprecedented effect, one which excited the enthusiasm of Berlioz. For the last twenty bars the voices intone the text *pp*, on the note C, and

the opening phrase (x) recurs again and again in the orchestra. The major mode establishes itself, then first the voices, afterwards the orchestra, merge into silence.

The success of the C minor Requiem was immediate and lasting. Beethoven affirmed that if he should write a Requiem, Cherubini's would be his only model. Schumann called it unequalled, Brahms marvellous. And many would agree with Berlioz's judgement that it is the composer's masterpiece. His second setting, the Requiem in D minor, was written in 1836, when the composer was in his seventy-sixth year. Much had happened in the intervening period. The closure of the Chapel Royal by Louis Philippe had left Cherubini without a regular incentive to compose. His duties as Director of the Conservatoire, carried out with punctilious conscientiousness, absorbed most of his energies. Consequently he had produced no major work—except the ill-starred *Ali Baba*, a remodelling of an earlier score—for more than a decade. His creative spirit seemed to have dried up, as he became an anachronism in the Paris of Meyerbeer and Berlioz, Bellini, Liszt, and Chopin. The companions of his youth disappeared one by one, and his thoughts turned increasingly to his own death. At the funeral of Catel, his colleague and friend for over thirty years, he exclaimed, 'Farewell for the last time, dearly beloved Catel! Perhaps I shall rejoin you before long.' In 1834 the Archbishop of Paris objected to the performance of the C minor Requiem at Boieldieu's funeral, as women's voices were included. Cherubini resolved to compose another Requiem for his own funeral, which would be exempt from this criticism, and he scored the D minor Requiem for men's voices and orchestra. His chorus comprises first and second tenors and basses. Thus a three-part texture predominates, although further division is frequent in the more chordal passages. The first tenor part is designed for that class of high tenor, approaching a counter-tenor, formerly common in France. This has two important consequences. Firstly, Cherubini can achieve fairly wide-spaced chords and textures. Secondly, the vocal ensemble is given a special intensity of tone colour, deriving from the high tessitura of the top part, and the masculine unity of the voices. (A similar colour characterizes the *Lamentations* of Tallis.)

This sound is matched in the Introit by the orchestral scoring: two bassoons, two horns, timpani, divided cellos, and basses, these being entirely independent of the cellos. In the instrumental prelude the cellos begin *pp* on a unison D, then divide. Their phrase, accompanied on the other instruments by off-beat chords, rises slowly to its climax, then falls back. The voices enter in imitation, their sinuous lines having a modal fluidity found elsewhere in the work (Ex. 44). The phrase 'et lux perpetua' arouses no musical response, as it did in the earlier setting. The chromaticism is intensified, and the resolution again on to D minor (Ex. 45). The Kyrie section begins in the major, with answering dialogue between the voices. They come together for the concluding statement, but the implications of their final D major chord are gently denied by the orchestral postlude, which returns to the minor.

Ex.44

Ex. 45

Four bars of introduction by bassoon, cellos and double basses lead to the entirely unaccompanied Graduale, sung, like the Kyrie, softly. Its chromatic progressions seem to hark back to Gesualdo. It is in A minor, and at the end the voices come to a pause on an A major chord. A flashing ascent by the upper strings, entering for the first time, on the dominant minor ninth, culminates in a *ff* outburst from the chorus, and full orchestral tutti (except trombones) on the words 'Dies irae'. This is an electrifying moment (Ex. 46). A return to *p* is maintained until reiterated A's, *ff*, announce the 'Tuba mirum'. Twice more the brass interrupt

Ex.46

31

the voices with their ominous summons. 'Mors stupebit' is treated quietly
and staccato, as in the C minor Requiem, but now 'judicanti' is emphasized
by a startling change of harmony. 'Judex ergo' is similarly underlined by
a new dotted rhythm and modulation. At 'Rex tremendae' there is a magnificent *ff* climax, to a broader tempo. (Ex. 47). The majestic vision gives

Ex. 47

way to anxious pleading at 'Salva me'. Another change of tempo, to a triple
time Andantino, occurs at 'Recordare'. Cherubini follows Mozart in
setting his text canonically, with the strings weaving a melancholy
counterpoint round the voices. 'Confutatis maledictis' is sung to short,
jagged phrases, doubled by the full orchestra, presto (Ex. 48). Violence
gives way to a quiet unaccompanied lento setting of 'Voca me'. The
ensuing 'Oro supplex' is remarkable in its harmonic progressions (Ex.
49). In the 'Lacrimosa' the falling unison phrases of the voices and
woodwind are supported by heavy trombone chords and stressed
appoggiaturas in the upper strings (Ex. 40). The weight of guilt is lifted
by the D major 'Pie Jesu'. But once again the orchestra refutes the
major conclusion.

The Offertorium (in F major) follows a similar pattern to that of the
C minor Requiem. The contrast of 'sed signifer Michael' is again

Ex.48

Ex.49

Ex.50

handled with the most sensitive colouring of the higher woodwind and strings. The first statement of 'Quam olim Abrahae' is here only eleven bars long. In the 'Hostias' the quiet homophony of the voices is adorned by a most expressive arabesque on the violins. The return of 'Quam olim' is much extended. Cherubini begins with imitations, as if he intended to write the usual fugue, and then changes to less contrapuntal treatment, whipping up the excitement by a not altogether convincing più mosso.

The Sanctus (in B♭ major) is more interesting than its predecessor of 1816. The divided strings produce a rich sound, and the quiet interlude of the Benedictus gives the violins yet another opportunity to embellish the vocal lines. The Pie Jesu is, like the Graduale, unaccompanied, except for a brief phrase on clarinets and bassoons framing it and linking its three statements. This is the most serene movement in the work. Its G minor opening phrase recurs in G major, and blossoms into a cadence of calm beauty (Ex. 51). This time the major mode remains uncontradicted.

Ex. 51

In the Agnus Dei, as before, the invocation is strong, the petition quiet, this time unaccompanied. There is a vigorous appeal on the words 'Lux aeterna luceat eis'. But the unaccompanied single lines of the 'quia pius es' reduce the music to the level of *pp*. Then begins a coda as original as that of the first Requiem. The voices intone on a D and an A. These two notes are sustained alternately by different woodwind instruments. The timpani contribute a two-bar motif, whose repetitions are spaced out by rests. A two-crotchet figure on the strings is slurred across the accented beats. A short crescendo leads to a broad final cadence for the voices, in D major. Then, for the third time in the work, the descending strings lapse into the minor mode, and the whole orchestra joins in the final *pp* chord.

Compared to the C minor Requiem, the D minor has been neglected, partly because of the difficulty presented by its choral disposition, but also because it is less immediately accessible than its companion work. In the C minor Requiem Cherubini is the spokesman for all mankind; in the D minor he is speaking for himself. The C minor is objective, consistent in idiom, coherent in form, traditional in its interpretation,

34

its major resolutions affirming the ultimate reconciliation of Christian hope. The D minor is introspective, widely varied in style, loose in structure, unorthodox in its profound pessimism. Both are true expressions of the paradoxical nature of their creator. The C minor is the work of the mature, self-confident master. The D minor is the utterance of the musical explorer who once described his own compositions as 'experiments, attempts to something better'; of the austere, passionate old man whose last words were, 'I do not wish to die.'

CHAPTER THREE

ORCHESTRAL MUSIC

IN all Cherubini's output there are only two full-scale orchestral works not connected with a stage production: the Overture in G major, and the Symphony in D major, both written during a visit to London in 1815, for performance by the recently founded Philharmonic Society. Neither of these commissioned works was successful. The overture, in the Italian style, is more notable for fullness of scoring and brilliance of effect than for quality of musical ideas. The symphony commands greater interest, partly because Italian nineteenth-century symphonies are rare. In it Cherubini did not attempt to emulate Haydn or Beethoven. His style is light, and in place of the rich counterpoint of the Austrian composers he frequently enlivens his texture with canonic imitation, as in the second idea from the first movement. Of the four movements the Scherzo is the best, for its vivacity and the instrumental colouring of its D minor trio. In the other movements Cherubini seems barely at ease in this new field, and, despite what some writers have suggested, the work is in no sense a synthesis of Italian lyricism and Teutonic strength. It was in a different category of orchestral composition that he made a major contribution to musical history.

In no other aspect of his work is the power and originality of Cherubini's genius more apparent than in the overtures to his operas. Their excellence was acclaimed by his contemporaries, and even a slight acquaintance with them reveals how deeply they must have imprinted themselves on the aural consciousness of the German romantics, Beethoven and Weber, Schubert and Mendelssohn. Cherubini's newly minted coinage quickly became European currency. The prime function of the overtures is, of course, 'to apprise the spectators of the nature of the following action', and they fulfil Gluck's impressive sounding but ambiguous object as well as those of any other composer, even when the expectations so aroused are subsequently deceived. If Wagner's assertion that the whole drama of *Les deux Journées* is contained within the overture is an exaggeration it is nevertheless true that the atmosphere of the overture is related closely to that of the opera, and the same may be said of *Eliza*, *Médée*, and *Ali Baba*. It is, however, as independent concert overtures that these compositions have survived, and the overtures to the eight full-scale operas composed after 1790, taken as a group, form a major contribution to the orchestral repertoire.

Nothing less than a detailed analysis of each work would do justice to the composer's range of thought. But an overall survey of the principal characteristics of the overtures may suggest some lines of approach. In order to see his achievement in perspective it is desirable to recall some of the features of the great contemporary school of instrumental composition centred in Vienna. Much emphasis has lately been laid on thematic relationships in classical structure. Important as these relationships undoubtedly are, the main structural factor in movements based on sonata-form is tonality rather than material. It was the tonal coherence of sonata-form that enabled composers to experiment with widely different thematic procedures. Haydn and Mozart did not tamper with the tonal principles of the form, and for that very reason had great freedom in the handling of theme and texture. The essentials of the form, as seen in Haydn and Mozart, are:

(1) An exposition establishing (a) the home key, (b) the second key: dominant or relative major
(2) A development or link passing through other keys
(3) A recapitulation, re-establishing the main key, with or without a coda

(1) The presentation of key in the exposition is purely structural. There is no attempt to impose a colour contrast, necessitating the introduction of a third, less closely related key.

(2) The development may be short or long. It may pass through a small or large number of tonal centres. There will be in any case a sense of tonal progression in the section; the same key will not be emphasized twice, and a repetition of a modulatory course, even when transposed, will be avoided.

(3) The return may be effected in different ways. It will be marked by the clear re-establishment of the home key, and a restatement in that key of most, if not all, of the material of the exposition. The recapitulation, together with the coda, if any, will be at least as long as the exposition.

The three sections thus have tonal functions which may be summarized:

(1) Establishment of home key, and motivation of further tonal activity by move to well-defined second centre

(2) Dramatic evolution of tonality by tonal movement and resultant key contrasts

(3) Restatement of home key, whose emphasis is increased by its absorption of material previously heard in second key

The thematic functions of the sections are usually closely related to their tonal functions. The material is stated in the exposition in two groups, corresponding to the two tonal areas. It is developed in the middle section, and restated more or less in its original guise in the recapitulation. This generalization is, however, subject to important modifications, especially in late Haydn, where the same material sometimes serves for both groups, and the thematic development continues through the recapitulation.

Cherubini's starting-point was not this mature form, but the Italian operatic overture or sinfonia, from which sonata-form originated. In the sinfonia the second key area is less strongly defined; the range of tonal movement and thematic development in the short middle section is very restricted; the return to the home key is not emphasized by a recapitulation of the material in its entirety. Discursive rather than dramatic, its elegant flow precludes the elements of contrast and tension. Yet it was these very elements that Cherubini was determined to introduce, and he did so by all the means at his disposal, through his treatment of tonality, material, texture, orchestration, and dynamics.

He began by prefacing each of his overtures, except *Médée* and *Ali Baba*, with an introduction of substantial proportions. All of these are notable, but two deserve special mention. In *Eliza*, after a tutti of thirteen bars, a pastoral theme is announced by violins and bassoons, with horn accompaniment (Ex. 52). Later on another figure develops on violins and horns (Ex. 53), and the repeated chord figure, *pp*, leads into

Ex. 52

Ex. 53

the Allegro spiritoso. The pastoral theme recurs in the second group, in a different form (Ex. 54).

Ex.54

The introduction to *Les deux Journées* must rank as one of the most original achievements in orchestral music. After thirty years it still made an overwhelming impression. 'The first three bars of the overture to *Les deux Journées*', wrote Mendelssohn in 1834, 'are worth more than our entire repertoire.' The mysterious descent of the cellos and basses introduced a 'frisson nouveau' into musical history (Ex. 55).

Ex.55

The main section of each overture is an Allegro, and Cherubini's divergence from Viennese methods manifests itself immediately. In *Médée* (written in F minor) he moves without tonal detour to the relative major, A♭. But in none of the other overtures, all in the major mode, does he reach the dominant major directly. *Ali Baba* (F major) is the nearest to orthodoxy; but even here he touches F minor first. In *Lodoiska* (D major) he announces a new theme in the dominant minor, before repeating it in the major (Ex. 56). In *Les Abencérages* (D major) he also introduces a dominant minor theme. This time, however, he proceeds to new material in the major. In *Les deux Journées* (E major) and *Faniska* (F major) he postulates the 'Terzverwandschaft' of the German theorists—the establishment of a key a third away from the tonic. The second group in *Les deux Journées* begins in G major, then moves to B major; that of *Faniska* begins in E♭ major, then moves to C major.

The two most remarkable expositions are those of *Eliza* (B♭ major) and *Anacréon* (D major). In *Eliza* Cherubini departs after two bars from his home key, passing through B♭ minor and D♭ major before arriving at a preparation for his dominant key. This preparation deceptively introduces the subdominant E♭ major, and it is some time before the dominant definitively arrives, with the theme quoted above in Ex. 54. In *Anacréon* the composer achieves the feat of arriving on dominant harmony, and persuading the listeners before leaving it that he is in the dominant key.

Ex.56

The structure of the remaining sections of the overtures is equally varied. In *Lodoiska* there is merely a brief link to an 'orthodox' recapitulation, with abbreviation of the first group and appropriate transposition of the second. *Médée*, *Les deux Journées*, *Faniska*, *Anacréon*, and *Ali Baba* all have short developments. That of *Anacréon* consists of a block of new material, repeated sequentially, and leading into the return of the tonic through a first inversion of C minor, the chord on the flattened seventh. The development of *Faniska* leads to a dominant preparation for a return of the relative minor—perhaps a subtle tribute to Haydn, who attended the first performance. In the recapitulation of *Anacréon* the second group is presented first. The same inversion occurs in *Médée*, giving an overall scheme of: Exposition: F minor—A♭ major; Development: B♭ minor. C minor; Recapitulation: F major— F minor; an ingenious solution to the problem of ending a minor movement with a major second group in the original mode. In *Eliza* and *Les Abencérages* the modulating development merges into a recapitulation in such a way that the home key is only established with the return of the material of the second group.

Four of the overtures have codas marked by a change of tempo. *Lodoiska* compensates for its previous regularity by a moderato section of forty-five bars, *pp* throughout, gently lyrical and romantic in its wind shadings, while the coda of *Eliza* provides a powerful confirmation of the somewhat neglected home key. The coda to *Anacréon* is the most remarkable of all. The return of the material from the second group is followed by the recall of a phrase from the introduction, with horn accompaniment. After a pause a new figure is introduced, accompanied by a variant of the horn motif. This latter undergoes further development, and then the main theme of the movement, until now absent from the recapitulation, is reintroduced. A virtuosic interplay of these

40

three ideas concludes the work, which well deserves Weber's enthusiastic comment: 'Champagnerleben!'

The interest in thematic interrelationship evinced in *Anacréon* is also evident elsewhere. *Médée*, for instance, provides an excellent example. A rhythmic feature 'x' of the passionate opening theme (Ex. 57) gives birth to a new idea, still in the first group (Ex. 58). In turn the

Ex.57

Ex.58

apparently subordinate figure 'y' assumes major significance in the passage that follows, and when the key of A♭ is reached, the principal idea of this second group is a condensation of the theme already heard. In *Les Abencérages* the opening idea and the material of the second group are related not only by their rhythmic similarity but by the antiphonal principle which governs them both. Here the orchestration plays a structural role in establishing a degree of identity (Exx. 59 and 60).

Ex.59

Ex.60

In Cherubini's orchestra the strings and double woodwind are invariable (with the second flute doubling piccolo in *Anacréon* and being replaced by it in *Ali Baba*). The brass section is subject to considerable variation, from the three horns of *Eliza* to the four horns, three trumpets and three trombones of *Ali Baba*. Whatever his forces, Cherubini deploys them with imaginative insight into the characteristics of the individual instruments, and a fine sense of balance and clarity in the tuttis. In some respects his conceptions were well ahead of his time. In the introduction to *Les deux Journées*, for example, the musical ideas depend entirely on their orchestration. Modern, too, is his manner of assisting his crescendi and diminuendi by gradual addition or withdrawal of his wind instruments. He uses dynamics to enhance the drama of his music in many ways, the most striking being his use of *p* and *pp*. At the opening of the Allegro in *Anacréon* a *pp*, enforced for forty-seven bars despite the build-up of the texture, lends the succeeding crescendo an explosive force.

From these general observations certain conclusions about the nature of Cherubini's achievement in the overtures may be drawn. Their tonal structure is much looser than that of sonata form. Tonal development begins in the exposition, and, although the dominant is eventually attained, its special relationship to the home key is blurred by the deviations preceding its appearance. Just as the exposition is tonally fluid, so, too, is the recapitulation. Moreover, no overall proportions exist between the sections, comparable to sonata form, and the effect is created of a freely evolving tonal pattern, anchored at each end in the home key. This tonal looseness is compensated for by two factors. Firstly, the composer's interest in thematic relationships, which gives his work a high degree of thematic unity. Secondly, his dramatic control, which enables him to organize widely contrasting musical ideas into a dramatically coherent whole.

It was the detail of Cherubini's overtures that most influenced his contemporaries: striking melodic phrases and modulations, new and startling orchestral ideas. The deeply subversive implications of his form had less effect on such composers as Beethoven and Schubert, grounded as they were on the rock of sonata-form, although Cherubini's example may have contributed to the widening of their sense of key relationships. It was a later school, that of Berlioz, Liszt, and Franck, who followed up his premises, subordinating structural to dramatic considerations, substituting thematic for tonal unity.

CHAPTER FOUR

CHAMBER, OCCASIONAL, AND DIDACTIC MUSIC

CHERUBINI'S first attempt at chamber-music composition, the six sonatas for keyboard written in 1780 at Milan, is of little importance. These works are indistinguishable from countless others composed in Italy at the time. They are all in two movements, the first in enlarged binary, the second in rondo form. The short-breathed ideas give way at the end of each section to the fashionable empty figuration. The minor mode is almost totally absent, and the harmony is excessively simple. A sonata for two organs, dating from the same year, has not survived.

There was no incentive to compose chamber music in late eighteenth-century France, and Cherubini's next venture, the two sonatas, or studies, for horn in F and string orchestra (1804) were written as exercises for use at the Conservatoire. They are among the first compositions for valved horn, and are available in a modern edition. The first sonata, a short Larghetto, is evidently designed to promote a cantabile style. Its companion piece is more wide ranging. The introductory Largo is an extended accompanied cadenza. It is followed by an Allegro moderato which tests the player's fluency and accuracy in such passages as Ex. 61. The Fantasia for organ or piano (1810) is chiefly remarkable for its chromatic harmony; it is not otherwise of interest.

Ex.61

Cherubini's most important group of chamber works is the set of six string quartets. The first, in E♭ major, was composed in 1814, although it remained unperformed until 1826. No. 2 in C is a transposition and reworking of the symphony, with a new slow movement, dating from 1829. The remaining four, in D minor, E major, F major and A minor, belong to the years 1834–7. Once again Cherubini embarked on a new compositional course without any external stimulus, and with few prospects of performance. Perhaps he found in quartet writing a relaxation from the more serious problems of church composition. So at any rate his reply to Hiller, who complimented him on them, would suggest: 'It passes the time and gives me pleasure, but I make no claims for them.' The enthusiasm of Hiller has been shared by others, including Hohenemser. Confalonieri sees the works as a bridge between the classical and romantic quartet. But admiration is by no means universal, and the quartets have been virtually ignored by chamber players, those most ruthlessly discriminating of musicians. Cherubini's personality and background did not predispose him to success in the medium. With the brilliant exception of Mozart, composers have rarely excelled in both chamber music and opera. The operatic composer communicates his feelings at one remove, through the realization of his characters; he works on a large-time scale, and the shape and character of his music is largely determined by extra-musical factors. The chamber composer communicates his feelings directly, working on a smaller canvas in exclusively musical terms. Cherubini was a man whose deepest feelings were always concealed from the gaze of others. He could project them into his characters, but he could not or would not reveal them in his chamber music. So it is the craftsman, and not the artist, who composed the quartets. The outer movements have soundness of structure, contrapuntal ingenuity and textural clarity and variety. But there is an inescapable impression of calculation, a coolness, at the very heart of the music. Formal weakness may be forgiven in chamber music, and often is in Schubert and Dvořák; indifference, never.

The slow movements are not much better in this respect. Confalonieri regards the main theme of the Adagio from the F major quartet as an idealized contact between Cherubini and Schubert. But the connexion is a formal one only; the sheer musical quality and intensity of feeling of Schubert is quite unmatched.

The best movements are the Scherzi. Here Cherubini's sense of instrumental colour provides the point of departure, and the style of these movements constantly recalls that of younger composers. Referring to the E♭ quartet, Robert Schumann praised the Scherzo with its 'Spanish theme' (Ex. 62) and its 'extraordinary trio', played *pp* throughout (Ex. 63). Hohenemser claims that the Scherzo of the A minor quartet could have been written note for note by Schumann himself, and the same observation could be applied to the themes of the Scherzi in the D minor and F major quartets. If performing etiquette allowed for the presentation of single movements in chamber recitals, these Scherzi would make an enjoyable if minor addition to the repertoire.

Ex.62

Ex.63

Cherubini's vocal chamber music falls into two categories, according to the language of the texts. His French 'romances', such as the eighteen on texts by Florian of 1787, are typical examples of the bergerette type. Among the Italian cantatas the most important is that composed for his London visit of 1815, *Inno alla Primavera*, for voices and orchestra. In four contrasting sections, it is virtuosic and tuneful in the Italian manner, without having any special distinction. More worthy of attention is a work which bridges the gap between chamber and occasional music. In 1805 a report of Haydn's death reached Paris. The false rumour gave rise to one of the best 'tombeaux' in French musical history. In his *Chant sur la mort de Haydn* Cherubini took for his text one of the pseudo-classical epitaphs popular in his day. A solo voice mourns in recitative 'tout se perd dans la nuit sans retour', and is answered by a trio asserting the creator's immortality 'comme son nom fameux, son âme est immortelle'. The most striking feature of the *Chant* is the orchestral prelude. Here the violas are divided à 2, the cellos à 4, thus giving two four-part string groups, one high, one low. After some sustained wind chords establish a mysteriously solemn mood, the muted cellos intone a lament, whose sombre colour anticipates the second Requiem (Ex. 64). The lament is then taken up by the higher string group, before the voices enter. The prelude is a moving tribute to the great master of string sonority.

This was not Cherubini's first memorial score. As an officially recognized composer in revolutionary France he had in 1797 set to

music a *Hymne funèbre sur la mort du Général Hoche,* by M. J. Chénier.
An extended funeral march introduces the four stanzas of the text.
The composition attained immediate popularity; it was staged at the
Opéra and at the Feydeau, and was used later, with appropriate textual
alterations, for the funeral of General Joubert. It is, by reason of its
instrumental introduction, the only one of the composer's revolutionary
hymns and songs that merits any notice. Cherubini's participation in
revolutionary propaganda was reluctant and limited. Like his colleagues
Gossec, Méhul, Lesueur, and Catel, he was not expected to exceed the
highest common factor of public taste and performing ability in this
field. Nor did the texts, impeccably patriotic though they were, excite
the musical imagination. That of *Le salpêtre républicain,* exhorting the
miners to greater efforts in defence of the Motherland, is representative.

> Lavez la terre en un tonneau
> En faisant évaporer l'eau
> Bientôt le nitre va paraître
> Pour visiter Pitt en bâteau
> Il ne nous faut que du salpêtre.

Rarely has Pegasus been more heavily handicapped.

It was at this time that Cherubini, appointed Inspector at the newly-
founded Conservatoire, inaugurated his output of didactic music, with
a collection of thirty-nine figured basses in 1798, and sixty-five solfeggi

in the following year. During the first two decades of the nineteenth century he compiled similar material at irregular intervals, and after his appointment as Director in 1822 he produced numerous short instrumental pieces for use at the annual examinations. But his principal contribution to musical training is the well-known *Cours de contrepoint et de fugue*, of 1835. This treatise, based on the works of such theorists as Fux, Marpurg, and Martini, was designed to guide the student through the five species of strict counterpoint to the composition of complete fugues. It is systematically laid out, its rules and observations supported by many illustrations, culminating in the eight-part fugue from Cherubini's own Credo, and its progenitor, that of Sarti. The *Cours* was translated into several languages, including English, and was widely used in academic institutions throughout Europe in the nineteenth century. Its popularity has done Cherubini's reputation more harm than good. Many students have assumed without personal knowledge that his compositions must be as dull as his exercises. None of the eighteenth-century theorists, however, confused the means, strict counterpoint, with the end, free composition. Counterpoint, as Cherubini said, is the grammar of music. It is easy in retrospect to see the limitations of eighteenth-century counterpoint teaching: the artificial separation of rhythms into species, the imposition of eighteenth-century diatonicism upon sixteenth-century modal procedures. But this method served an invaluable function in its day. It was this training in strict counterpoint as much as anything else that enabled Haydn and Mozart to break through the equally restricting conventions of the 'style galant' to the textural richness and motivic interplay of their last works. And to attribute the lack of inspiration of the Victorian composers to an excessive concentration on academic counterpoint is to mistake effect for cause. No great composer yet has been stifled by contrapuntal study. Schumann, one of the best contrapuntists as well as one of the most spontaneous geniuses of his century, derived a great deal of benefit from Cherubini's text-book: and that alone would justify its existence.

CHAPTER FIVE

THE MAN

OUTSIDE the work of his biographers, Cherubini has by and large not enjoyed a very good press, for a variety of reasons. Much of what is written about music, that universal language, has a distinctly local bias. It is Cherubini's misfortune that he has never had prestige value as the embodiment of a national tradition. His work falls between two great periods of Italian music, and the best of it is outside the Italian operatic sequence altogether. His adopted country, which he served so long and so well, has repaid him badly. The fact that so much of their music has been written or influenced by foreigners is a permanent source of disquiet to French historians. Confronted with the inescapable pre-eminence of Lully, they have been reluctant to acknowledge the role of the later Florentine, and they prefer to regard him as a disciple of Méhul. The charge of imitation was first laid by a critic after the première of *Médée*, and Méhul himself, that most generous of men and loyal of friends, replied in an open letter to the Paris press: ' . . . *Le Censeur* continues and says "here there are reminiscences and imitations of Mehul". Is it to Cherubini of all people that this reproach is directed? To Cherubini, the most original, the most fertile among our musicians? O *Censeur*, you do not know this great artist! But I know him well. I assert and will prove to all Europe that the inimitable author of *Démophon*, of *Lodoiska*, of *Eliza* and of *Médée* has no need of imitation to be elegant or sensitive, graceful or tragic. . . .' Sometimes grudging recognition is seasoned with discreet character assassination. In *L'Age Classique de la Musique Française* (Paris, 1948) Bernard Champigneulle mentions Cherubini with Paisiello and Lesueur as precursors of Berlioz, and adds a footnote: 'It is interesting to note that Paisiello, the first official composer of the Empire, and Cherubini, the one who occupied with adaptability (*souplesse*) the highest administrative functions under the diverse régimes which succeeded one another at the beginning of the century, were also Italians.' This portrait of a musical Vicar of Bray contrasts strongly with the reality of Cherubini's repeated defiance of Napoleon.

Only the Germans, ever willing to confer honorary nationality on any artist of whom they approve, have sometimes given Cherubini credit where it is due. And even their attitude has been complicated by Cherubini's relationship to Beethoven.

There can be no evasion of Beethoven's unswerving admiration for Cherubini. In 1805 he called the Italian Europe's foremost dramatic composer. Twelve years later, asked whom he considered to be the greatest living composer, he answered: 'Cherubini.' He was always interested in news of Cherubini's work, and among his papers was the German draft of a letter to Cherubini, in which he said he would be honoured by a reply. Years later Cherubini told Beethoven's biographer Schindler that he never received the letter. Schindler, passionately devoted to the creation of the Beethoven legend, did not give Cherubini the benefit of the doubt, and so the picture of the cold academician, indifferent to the unmerited devotion of the misunderstood genius, gradually took shape. In fact, as Schemann and Confalonieri have shown, Cherubini apparently reciprocated Beethoven's esteem, and certainly he actively promoted his music in France. As to the influence of Cherubini on Beethoven's music—a far-reaching subject which cannot be dealt with in a short space—it has been minimized by reputable historians anxious to preserve the purity of the Austro-German succession. Thus Marx: 'That the "eclectic" . . . provided the model for *Leonore* is just not true . . . Beethoven is the successor of Haydn and Mozart.'

Much more damaging to Cherubini's reputation were his contacts with another composer of genius. Berlioz, like Wagner, combined exceptional artistic integrity with an infinite capacity for self-delusion in personal matters. Berlioz the critic praised, sometimes most generously, the music of Cherubini. Berlioz the autobiographer, seeking someone to play the arch-villain in the melodrama of his life, chose the Director of the Conservatoire, Member of the Institute, and author of the *Cours de Contrepoint*. The young student's revolt against the official teaching and policy of the Conservatoire was understandable, indeed necessary. But the spectacle of the mature composer of the *Grande Messe des Morts* and *Les Troyens* setting out in his *Mémoires* to deface the posthumous image of the creator of the two Requiems and *Médée*, by an ingeniously compounded mixture of gossip, truth, half-truth, and lies, is not an edifying one.

Besides these factors, however, there remains the personality of the man himself. Cherubini was that most difficult of types, a conservative revolutionary. This prophet of romanticism, who anticipated the nineteenth-century concept of music drama, who inaugurated a formal revolution and discovered new orchestral sonorities, belonged in his ideals and his conduct to the eighteenth century. He was as dedicated to his art as any romantic; but he approached it as a craftsman, not a priest. He published no pamphlets, uttered no oracles, wrote no criticism or memoirs. He had a profound love of order and convention in daily life, and, like Lord Shaftesbury, disapproved of enthusiasm. Flattery he disliked; he had a clear sense of his own limitations, and would not allow admirers to place him among the immortals. When asked if he intended to dedicate the score of *Les deux Journées* to Haydn he replied that he had not written anything worthy of that great master. He felt deeply, but believed that feeling was private. In his later years especially he developed a protective armour against intrusions. He sought, and acquired, a reputation for inaccessibility. But, as many musicians found out, his defences were easily penetrated. Spohr's experience was not uncommon. 'The old gentleman', he wrote in his autiobiography, 'welcomed me without introduction of any kind, in the most friendly manner possible, and invited me to come and see him again as often as I might wish.'

One of the most vivid contemporary accounts of him is that of Adolphe Adam, in his *Derniers souvenirs d'un musicien*:

'Extremely highly-strung, abrupt, irritable, completely independent, his first reactions were nearly always unfavourable. He quickly regained his natural disposition, which was excellent, and which he tried to conceal under the most forbidding exterior. So, despite his unevenness of temper (some maintained that his temper was very even, because he was always angry), he was worshipped by those who were close to him. The veneration of his pupils approached fanaticism. Mm. Halévy and Batton tended him in his last hours with filial care. Boieldieu always spoke of him with respect and tenderness, and Cherubini returned to his pupils all the affection that they felt towards him. One above all, Halévy, he regarded as one of his own children. Less than a month ago, speaking to me of this beloved pupil, he expressed his feelings with such fervour that I was moved to tears.

'The reactions one experienced when meeting him were so strange that it is difficult to define, let alone understand them. The veneration one felt for his great age and his fine talents was changed abruptly by the absurdity of the minutiae to which he clung with obstinate persistence. Then, after a little, as though he realised that he was wasting too much time in contrariness, his face cleared, the sensitive, mischievous smile that he could use when he chose, animated his fine old face; good nature prevailed, the spoilt child disappeared, and he grew kindly in spite of himself. He opened his heart to you, and then you could resist him no longer; you took your leave enchanted, amazed at having felt for this extraordinary man, in so short a time, such a variety of emotions: admiration, revulsion, and attraction. In a word, you have seen how easily your own nature adapted itself to his, and almost in spite of him you have been unable to stop yourself from liking him.'

Among the musicians who visited the composer regularly at his apartment in the rue Poissonière were Rossini and Chopin. One friendship in particular had a special meaning for him in his latter days. He made the acquaintance of Ingres in the late 1820s, and a warm bond of sympathy developed between the two artists, whose aims and conceptions were in many respects similar. They were united by their reciprocal interests. Cherubini practised his painting under Ingres's guidance, and together they played and talked of music. Their meetings ceased in 1831, when Ingres went to Italy. On his return ten years later the ageing composer welcomed him eagerly and consented to sit for a portrait. In his superb painting, now in the Louvre, Ingres portrayed with profound undestanding the tired but indomitable old man; the face, with its sunken cheeks, veiled eyes, and set, down-turned mouth, still bears the traces of the poetic sensibility which distinguished the composer in his youth. Unknown to Cherubini, the artist added the figure of a muse saluting the composer. Thinking to surprise and please his friend, Ingres invited him to view the completed portrait in his studio. Cherubini came, looked at it in silence, turned on his heel and walked out. It was not for Ingres to decide where and when the accolade of the muses should be awarded, he told his family, and retired in a fury to his study. Meanwhile the dismayed painter had dispatched a note of apology to Mme Cherubini, which Halévy later took in to his teacher. Some time later Cherubini emerged with a sheet of manuscript, inscribed

Canon in three voices. Justice due to his excellent gifts, in friendship for dear Ingres, from his grateful admirer, Luigi Cherubini.

The composer's text began:

O Ingres amabile,
pittor chiarissimo . . .

Thus, with a gesture of reconciliation to a friend, and a tribute to a fellow artist, Cherubini completed his working life. Two months later, on the fifteenth of March 1842, he died.

BIOGRAPHICAL SUMMARY

1760 15 September. Luigi Carlo Zanobi Salvatore Maria Cherubini born in Florence.

1766 Begins musical studies with his father, harpsichordist at the Teatro alla Pergola.

1773 First compositions recorded in composer's own *Catalogue*, a Mass and Intermezzo.

1778 Begins study with Sarti in Bologna, later in Milan.

1780 First opera *Il Quinto Fabio* performed in Alessandria.

1781 Completes his studies, returns to Florence.

1784 Leaves for London, via Paris.

1785 *La finta principessa*, opera buffa, performed in London.

1786 *Il Giulio Sabino*, opera seria, in London.

1787 Takes up residence in Paris.

1788 *Ifigenia in Aulide*, his last opera seria, performed in Turin. *Démophon*, first French opera, performed in Paris.

1789 Becomes musical director of the Théâtre de Monsieur, founded for performance of opera buffa in Paris.

1791 Théâtre de Monsieur moves to rue Feydeau. *Lodoiska* performed there.

1794 *Eliza.*

1795 Paris Conservatoire founded. Five 'Inspectors' appointed: Lesueur, Grétry, Gossec, Méhul, Cherubini. Marries Cécile Tourette.

1797 *Médée.*

1798 *L'Hôtellerie portugaise.*

1800 *Les deux Journées.*

1802 *Lodoiska, Eliza, Médée,* and *Les deux Journées (Der Wasserträger)* performed in Vienna.

1803 *Anacréon.*

1805 Visits Vienna. Meets Haydn, Beethoven, Hummel, Grillparzer.

1806 *Faniska* written and performed in Vienna.

1808 Visits to Chimay. Mass in F begun.

1809 Mass in F completed. *Pimmalione.*

1810 *Le Crescendo.*

1811 Mass in D minor.

1813 *Les Abencérages.*

1814 Created Chevalier of the Légion d'Honneur. Appointed Superintendent of the Chapel Royal. First String Quartet.

1815 Becomes member of the Institute. Visit to London, at the invitation of
the Philharmonic Society. Composes for the occasion Overture in
G major, Symphony in D major, cantata *Inno alla Primavera.*

1816 Mass in C major, Requiem in C minor. Composes numerous Latin
motets in this and the following years.

1819 Mass in G major, intended for coronation of Louis XVIII, which did
not take place.

1822 Appointed Director of the Conservatoire.

1825 Mass in A major, for the coronation of Charles X.

1833 *Ali-Baba.*

1836 Requiem in D minor.

1837 Sixth and last String Quartet.

1842 Created Commander of the Légion d'Honneur. Dies 15 March.